TO BE A UNICORN

TO BE A UNICORN

ROBERT VAVRA
AND
FLEUR COWLES

William Morrow & Company, Inc.
New York

Library of Congress Cataloging-in-Publication Data

Vavra, Robert.
To be a unicorn.

Summary: An illustrated poem about the
perceived barriers that frustrate the
love of a mare and a unicorn.
1. Unicorns—Poetry. [1. Unicorns—Poetry.
2. Horses—Poetry. 3. American poetry] I. Cowles,
Fleur. II. Title.
PS3572.A96T6 1986   811'.54   86-8572
ISBN 0-688-06598-8

Printed in the United States of America

First Edition

1 2 3 4 5 6 7 8 9 10

BOOK DESIGN BY BERNARD SCHLEIFER

*We thank the art and imagination of William Shakespeare,
Joseph Russegger, W.H. Auden, Roy Campbell, Charles M. Doughty,
Anne Morrow Lindbergh, Ralph Waldo Emerson, John Keats,
Henry King, William Wordsworth, Robert Browning, Francis
Lucien, T.H. White, Nathaniel Hawthorne, Percy Bysshe Shelley,
and William Jay Smith.*

FLEUR ·85·

A horse or not
    a horse
was not the question.

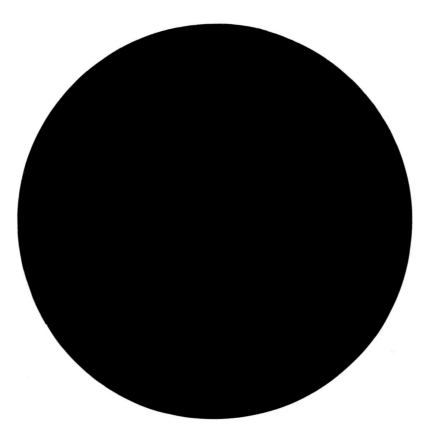

Seeing is believing
and that misty morning
in the glade I saw
Equus in Latin
Caballo in español.
I who hear no
    speak no
    see no evil
Should have known the being
    behind that image

was purer than the monkey business of
even
my imagination.

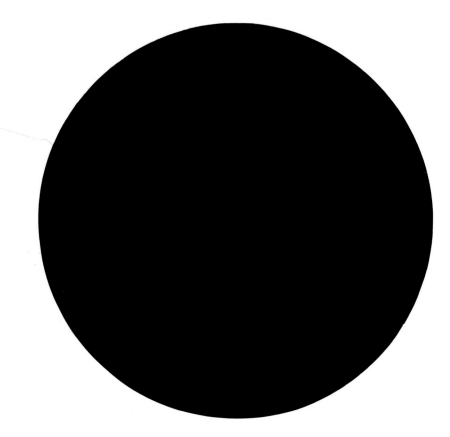

The self-armed steed
    the unicorn
Ever heard of never seen
White childhood moving like a sigh
Through the green woods unharmed in
your sophisticated innocence.
He,
single-horned Prince of purity
is the hero of my tale.

While night to his day,
Bitted, saddled
and sugar cube–rewarded,
A horse!
A horse!
My kingdom
for a horse!
is the unlikely
heroine
of this adventure.
No Black Beauty or Flicka
awaits
behind the barn door
     across
       the page.

She was just
a mare
in a stall
whose hay-chewing
uneventful life
was feeling
heels in her sides
and
"Get-eee-up"
and
"Whoooooo!"
in her ears.

But what is
a mare's life
but that of a chimp
in a cage
unless
she be one of those
Silver runaways
of
Neptune's car
Racing,
Spray curled
like waves
before
the wind.

She did not
dream
of winning
the Grand National
or
the Kentucky Derby
or of being painted
by Velasquez
or of Sunday's
standing
in bronze
in some city park.
She merely stood
in the imagination
of her
stall
which today
was
a poppy field
that brightened
red
some Spanish landscape.

When at first she saw
     him
she saw an
     equine
like herself

all shining beautiful
and gentle of himself

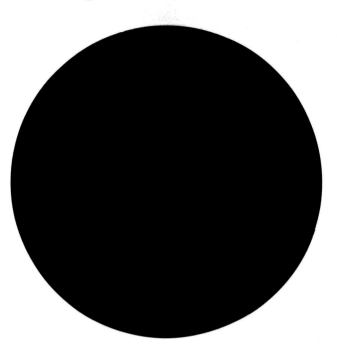

he seemed
a darling life
in that tide of pollen
not worthy of his delicate hoofs:
the strutting tail
flowed even
to
the ground,
and his mane
had been
arranged
by the loving hand
of
mother nature.

But,
bursting from
his tranquil brow

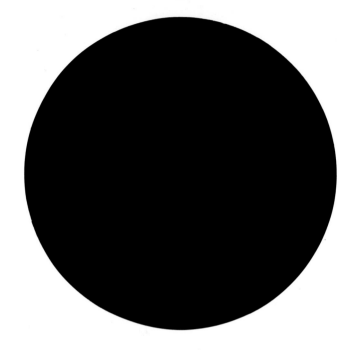

Springing
like
a lily white
To a longed for
    height
Or a fountain
    bright
Spurting
    light
Of early mourn—
Was a luminous
    horn!

"I am the owner
of the sphere;
Of the seven stars
and
the solar year,"
whispered
the unicorn.
"Of Caesar's hand
and Plato's brain.
Of Lord Christ's
heart
and
Shakespeare's
strain."
And as quickly
as the breeze
carried away
his words
he

       was

           gone.

"Without a horn,"
thought the mare,
"I'll always be
ridden and driven
never written
about
in songs
and bedtime stories.
But if
from my brow
were to spring
a radiant horn!
There would be sonnets
in which he and I
would be written
    'always'
since unicorns are
forever."

"I have stripes
yet
I love no tigress,"
brayed the zebra.
"Love needs not
its own
reflection
but only
love
in return.
Change my stripes
to win you
fair mare
would be like
the chimp
wishing for a tail
to sweep
from her branch
a monkey queen."

"I would be in heaven,"
whinnied the horse,
"if only I had
a
spiral
of
ivory
for a crown."

"A leopard can't
change his spots,"
purrrrrrred the cheetah.
"Beauty is truth,
truth beauty
that's all you know
on earth
and all you need
to know."

"And beauty am I!
You!
We!
All are beauty!"
proclaimed
the peacock.

"Perhaps your
one-horned king
seeks
a crownless queen.
Learn from the
timeless romance

of bees and butterflies
with flowers.
Oh,
if only we could
be as glorious as they,
yet so little vain.

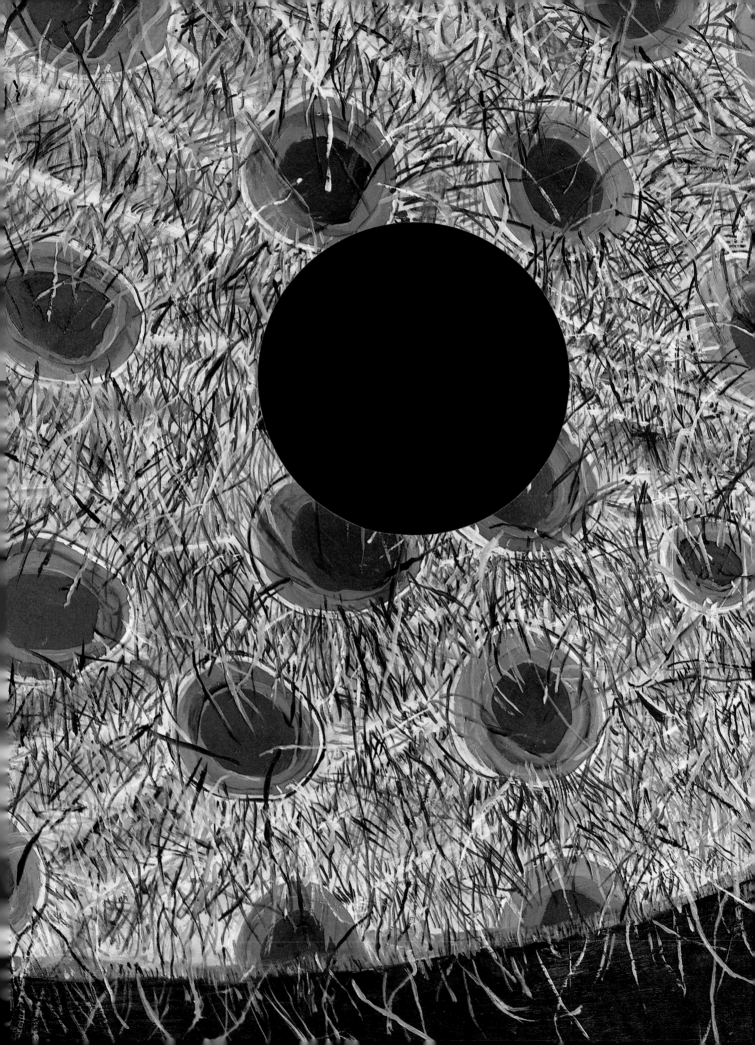

"The year's at
the Spring,"
echoed the peacock,
"and days at
the morn,
the hill-side's
    dewpearled,
The lark's on
the wing;
The snail's in
the thorn;
God's in
his heaven.
All's
    right
    with
    the
    world!"

FLEUR. 85

Black and white
flashed
again
the zebra's stripes
as did his words,
"Forget
your crown
of rainbows.
Instead garland
his horn
with wild sweet
flowers.
Frolic together
in
the Pasture,
for you've
long
enough endured
the
desire
of this summer day."

Then suddenly,
white with hooves
of silver
and graceful horn
of pearl
stood
before her
the proud
rebellious
unicorn.
The glorious thing
about him
was not his horn
but
his eyes
which were so
sorrowful,
lonely,
gently
and nobly tragic
that they killed
all other emotions
except
    love.

And as
gaze
met gaze
they felt
as
wild
and
swift,
and as
buoyant
in their
flight
through
the air,
as any eagle
that ever
        soared
into
the clouds.

Together they
went
into
the field
to take what
that sweet
hour
would
yield,
Where
all things
seem
only
one
in the universal sun.

They galloped
    across
    the forest green
    So quickly
    they were hardly seen
Where peacocks their blue feathers preen
    And
    strawberries
    grow
    wild.

OWNERSHIP OF PAINTINGS